Contents

Some words are shown in bold, **like this**.
You can find them in the glossary on page 23.

What is a narwhal?

A narwhal is a **mammal** that lives in icy **polar** waters.

All mammals have some hair on their bodies and feed their babies milk.

A Day in the Life: Polar Animals

Narwhal

Katie Marsico

www.raintreepublishers.co.uk
Visit our website to find out
more information about
Raintree books.

To order:
☎ Phone 0845 6044371
🖷 Fax +44 (0) 1865 312263
🖳 Email myorders@raintreepublishers.co.uk

Customers from outside the UK please telephone +44 1865 312262

Raintree is an imprint of Capstone Global Library Limited,
a company incorporated in England and Wales having its
registered office at 7 Pilgrim Street, London, EC4V 6LB
– Registered company number: 6695582

Text © Capstone Global Library Limited 2012
First published in hardback in 2012
First published in paperback in 2013
The moral rights of the proprietor have been asserted.

Edited by Daniel Nunn, Rebecca Rissman, and Sian Smith
Designed by Joanna Hinton-Malivoire
Picture research by Hannah Taylor
Original illustrations © Capstone Global Library
Production by Victoria Fitzgerald
Originated by Capstone Global Library Ltd
Printed and bound in China by South China Printing
Company Ltd

ISBN 978 1 406 22885 4 (hardback)
15 14 13 12 11
10 9 8 7 6 5 4 3 2 1

ISBN 978 1 406 22892 2 (paperback)
16 15 14 13 12
10 9 8 7 6 5 4 3 2 1

**British Library Cataloguing in Publication
Data**
Marsico, Katie, 1980-
    Narwhal. -- (A day in the life. Polar animals)
    1. Narwhal--Juvenile literature.
    I. Title II. Series
    599.5'43-dc22

Acknowledgements
We would like to thank the following for permission to
reproduce photographs: Corbis p. 6 (Paul Nicklen); FLPA pp.
4 (Minden Pictures/ Flip Nicklin), 7, 23c (Minden Pictures/
Flip Nicklin), 11 (Minden Pictures/ Flip Nicklin), 12 (Minden
Pictures/ Flip Nicklin), 17 (Sunset), 19 (Minden Pictures/ Flip
Nicklin), 22 (Minden Pictures/ Flip Nicklin); Getty Images
pp. 5, 23g (Paul Nicklen), 8, 23b (Paul Nicklen), 9 (Rudi
Sebastian), 16 (Minden Pictures/Flip Nicklin), 18 (Minden
Pictures/Flip Nicklin), 20, 23d (Minden Pictures/ Flip Nicklin),
21 (Minden Pictures/Flip Nicklin); Photolibrary pp. 13, 23f
(Waterframe Images), 14 (Robert Harding), 15 (Oxford
Scientific/Doug Allan); SeaPics.com pp. 10, 23a (© John K.B.
Ford/Ursus).

Front cover photograph of a narwhal and back cover
photograph of a narwhal's tusk reproduced with permission of
Getty Images (Paul Nicklen). Back cover photograph of a tail
reproduced with permission of Corbis (Paul Nicklen).

The publisher would like to thank Michael Bright for his
assistance in the preparation of this book.

tusk

Narwhals are whales.

Males have a long tooth called a **tusk** on their upper jaw.

What do narwhals look like?

tail

Narwhals have flippers and a tail.

Most have spotted skin.

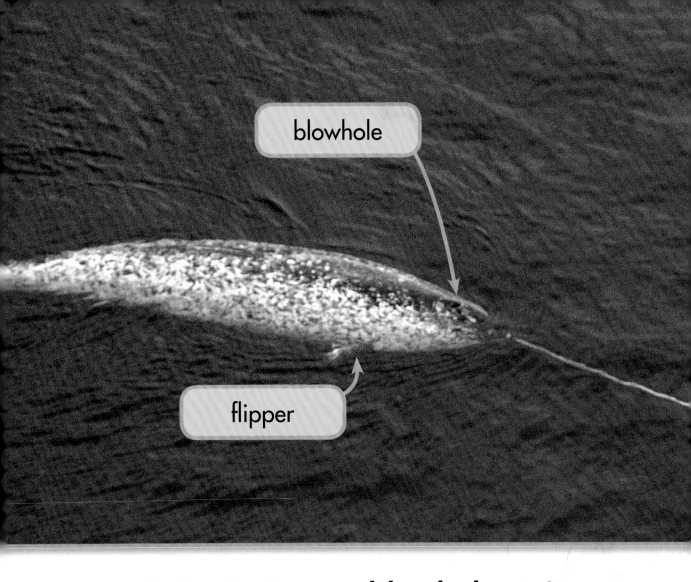

blowhole

flipper

Narwhals also have a **blowhole** at the top of their head.

They use the blowhole to breathe in air at the surface of the water.

Where do narwhals live?

Arctic

Narwhals live in the **Arctic**.

In the Arctic it is light all day and all night for part of the summer.

In the Arctic it is dark all day and all night for part of the winter.

The Arctic is one of the coldest places in the world!

What do narwhals do in the day?

Narwhals are **active** during the day and at night.

They spend part of the day searching for food deep in the ocean.

Narwhals spend some time resting near the surface of the water.

They need to breathe in air before they dive down to search for food.

What do narwhals eat?

fish

Narwhals eat fish, shrimp, and squid.

They often catch their food deep in the ocean, where it is very dark.

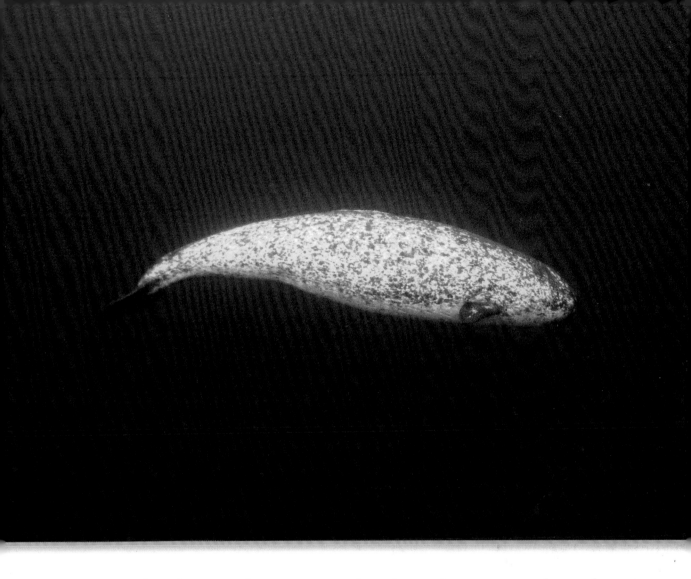

Narwhals make sounds that bounce back and tell them where things are.

This is called **sonar**.

What hunts narwhals?

killer whale

Killer whales hunt and eat narwhals.

Polar bears and walruses also attack them.

People hunt narwhals, too.

They kill the whales for their **tusks** and skin.

Do narwhals live in groups?

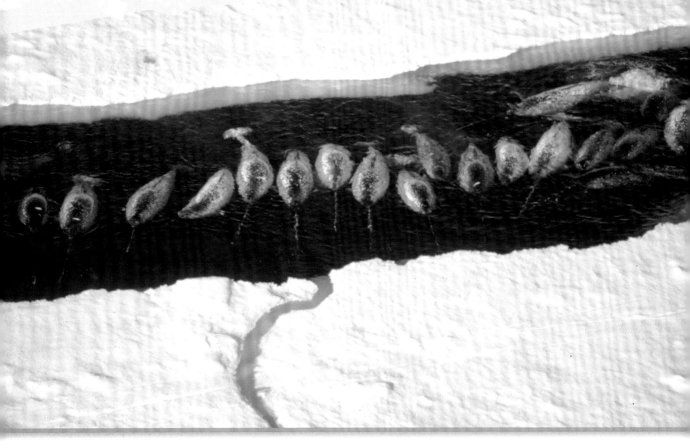

Narwhals live in groups called pods.

This helps them to keep safe from their enemies.

There are usually about 15 to 20 narwhals in a pod.

Narwhals travel together and communicate by using sounds such as clicks and whistles.

What do narwhals do at night?

Narwhals spend a lot of the night diving for food.

They can dive down into very deep parts of the ocean.

Narwhals sometimes rest in between dives at night, just as they do in the day.

People are still trying to find out more about how narwhals sleep.

What are baby narwhals like?

calf

A mother narwhal gives birth to a baby about once every three years.

Baby narwhals are called calves. They are a blue-grey colour.

A calf lives with its mother for one or two years while it drinks her milk.

Then young narwhals are ready to join a pod and go hunting in icy waters!

Narwhal body map

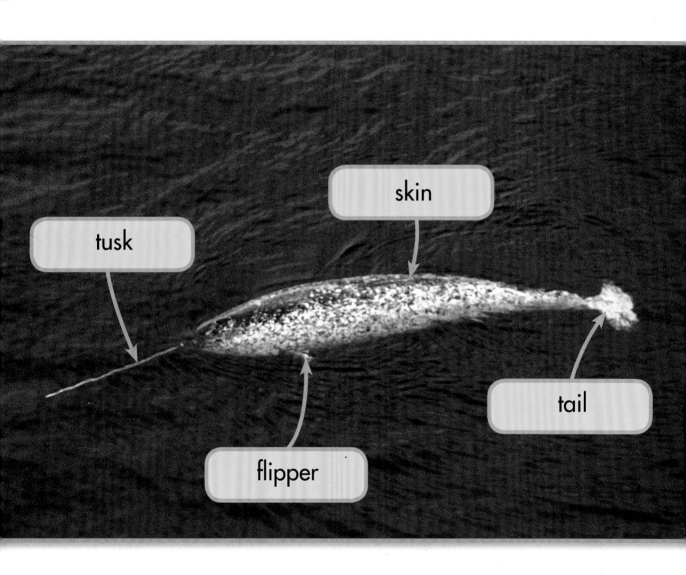

tusk

skin

flipper

tail

Glossary

active busy doing lots of things

Arctic area surrounding the North Pole. It is very cold in the Arctic.

blowhole hole at the top of a narwhal's head used for breathing air

mammal animal that feeds its babies milk. All mammals have some hair or fur on their bodies.

polar extremely cold areas at the top and bottom of the world

sonar a system that uses sound to find objects

tusk long, pointed tooth

Find out more

Books

Arctic and Antarctic (Eye Wonder), Lorie Mack (DK Publishing, 2006)
Whales of the Arctic, Sara Swan Miller (PowerKids Press, 2009).

Websites

video.kids.nationalgeographic.com/video/player/kids/animals-pets-kids/wild-detectives-kids/wd-ep4-narwhaltooth.html
Watch a video of narwhals on the National Geographic website.

www.sciencenewsforkids.org/articles/20060125/Feature1.asp
Find out about a narwhal's tooth at Science News for Kids.

Index